# Dr. Troy Clark's

## Lead Creation Scripts ©

for

## Final Expense Life Insurance

~ Field Agent or Phone Agent ~

Copyright © 2011 Dr. Troy G. Clark. All rights reserved.

Writings contained herein are from the author unless otherwise referenced.

**No part of this publication may be reproduced**, stored in a retrieval system or transmitted in any way by any means -electronic, mechanical, photocopy, recording or otherwise - without prior permission from Dr. Troy Clark.

DISCLAIMER: The information provided in this sales manual is not legal advice and does not guarantee satisfactory results for individual agents or agencies who employ any information herein to their own sales technique. All information provided is a suggestion, and may or may not be the best suggestion for the sales techniques and scenarios any agent encounters. Any user - person/agent/agency/corporation - who utilizes any part of this sales manual is 100% solely responsible for their own individual or corporate sales performances and sales technique decisions while utilizing this sales manual. Be fully aware and abide by governing laws and ethics. Every customer is to always be treated by an agent with utmost respect, dignity, and complete honesty.

More publications by Dr. Troy Clark: amazon.com/author/troyclark

### The secret to selling is to *sell the secret.* ©

Explaining your product should sound like the
"best kept secret"
in the entire insurance industry.
Make qualifying for one of your plans a
"mystery of anticipation."

**Troy Clark, PhD**

# Life ♦ Insurance

1809, Noun

Providing payment of a stipulated sum
to a designated beneficiary
upon death of the insured.

**Merriam-Webster's Dictionary**
11th Collegiate Version 3.0, 2003

# Professional Sales Pointers

*Because this Lead Creation Script is to be adapted to field or phone sales for salesmen-women, please consider the following additional pointers to owning a superior lead script:*

- A customer's reaction to an agent typically mirrors an agent's own disposition. That is, what an agent transfers over the phone, or in person, to a customer, is mostly how a customer treats an agent. If an agent exudes an unenthusiastic, low-droning voice, or frustrated disposition, the customer will react to the agent with a low interest level of enthusiasm, or negative disinterest. If an agent treats his/her customer to enthusiastic, professional, upbeat positivity and cheer, a customer is more likely to "perk up", pay attention, and listen with interest.

- RECORD YOURSELF verbalizing a lead script to a "pretend customer". Listen to your recording. Would you believe YOU? If not, why should your customer? Always improve **how you sound** while delivering a sales presentation!

- Because typical customers need professional assistance to overcome procrastination, seniors without any, or little, life insurance coverage put their family at risk of an approximate $7-$12,000 immediate funeral bill, if they should pass away at any moment.

- Many people living on savings, Social Security, or Disability, are unable to afford large, expensive-type life insurance plans. Helping folks to make a right decision that would fit into their individual lifestyle and budget is important. A large funeral bill, outstanding credit card debts, nursing care bills, etc., puts financial stress on a surviving spouse or children of the deceased. Final Expense life insurance is a wonderful way to individually eliminate this burden on an entire family creating an instant estate of cash benefits.

- In this Lead Creation Script, the term "Licensed Field Underwriter" should only be utilized by an agent while serving life insurance products who has previously secured permission from an insurance carrier to do so. Otherwise, replace the term "Licensed Field Underwriter" with "Final Expense Representative".

# Sales Techniques to Avoid

1. **Twisting** involves convincing a client to replace an existing policy, or switch insurance companies, through misrepresenting the existing policy's terms and values. Never tell a prospective client that your policy benefits will do something, knowing that it will not do it. Never tell a prospective client that their existing policy will not do something without reviewing their actual policy first.
2. A **Rebate** is illegal for both the agent and the consumer. An inducement offered (anything of value) not specified in the agent's policy contract within an insurance purchase agreement is a rebate. It is illegal for any person to offer or accept such an inducement.
3. An agent may not charge in excess of the policy premium for the performance of the agent's service.
4. It is also a misdemeanor to the agent in most states to transact a contract that is unlawfully executed. That is, soliciting and transacting business with a non-licensed company.
5. Knowingly making false statements on an application is punishable in most states as a Class I felony. This includes insurance agents, physicians in charge of medical checks, or applicants of life insurance. A blank application cannot be signed legally by an agent. Exceptions may be travel accident insurance, or a baggage loss policy, intended for issuance through a coin-operated machine.
6. Refrain from "hustling" or "badgering" a customer with untrue or unkind remarks, i.e.: "This is your last chance to ever qualify for these benefits", "Don't be a fool, sign up today", "If you wait another day to apply for this coverage, your chance will be lost forever."
7. Inherent within the insurance industry, unfortunately, are licensed agents whose only concern is to position a potential client to "sign on the dotted line" at all cost. To do so, a dishonest agent may withhold important, deal breaking information from the customer about a certain policy feature that may influence the customer's decision one way or another. For example, if a plan for coverage has a 2-3 year "waiting period" before 100% of the natural death benefits goes into full force, the customer should know this up front during the initial explanation of the benefits. If the "waiting period" is not properly and thoroughly explained at the time of purchase by the sales agent, a family may get surprised by the sting of having a fraction or zero coverage they were counting on, if the client passes away during the 2-3 year "waiting/elimination period". Up front honesty by the agent always wins more success in the long run.
8. Misrepresenting your product, or the product of another company that a customer is currently insured with, is detrimental to both parties involved and is no way to begin a lifelong, trusting business relationship. A customer is more likely to buy from a forthright, honest agent, who holds nothing back from the customer. There must be no "surprises" later to the customer or agent. On the flip side of this coin is manipulating a customer to buy insurance based upon untrue or over-the-top explanations of policy benefits. An agent must never promise a customer that their policy will do something that it will not do. We officially term this "twisting" of the facts in insurance terminology. If a professional agent is unsure how to explain policy benefits, or how to answer a customer's question about benefits, a correct response would be:

> "That's a good question. Let me make sure I can give you an accurate answer by looking it up for you. Because I am a professional, I do not want either of us to be surprised later by giving you a guess answer. We'll come back to that later, I promise."

**An Insurance Commissioner may revoke, suspend, or deny licensure to any individual for:**
- Cheating on the State Licensing Exam.
- Fraud. Coercive or dishonest practices.
- Misrepresentation of policy terms.
- Violation of any insurance law.
- Misappropriation of funds. Forging names on an application.
- Conviction involving moral turpitude or any felony.
- Violation of the Unfair Trade Practice.
- Failure to comply with continuing education requirements.

# Table of Contents

**Professional Sales Pointers** ............................................................. 3

**Sales Techniques to Avoid** .............................................................. 4

**LIVE Transfer Lead, "Fronter" Script** ............................................. 6
**LIVE Transfer Lead, "Closing Agent" Script** .................................. 8

**Predictive Lead, DIALER Script** .................................................... 13
**Predictive Lead, AGENT Script** ..................................................... 15

**Cold Call Lead** ................................................................................ 16

**Appointment Setting Lead** ............................................................ 17

**Voicemail Lead** ............................................................................... 18

**Answering Machine Agent Phone Message** ............................... 19

**NOTES** ............................................................................................ 21

# LIVE Transfer Lead, "Fronter" Script

*A "marketing agent", or "fronter", prequalifies each customer first before transferring customer to a "closing agent". Customer contact info is initially acquired through a cold call list, mailers, or top FE call centers generate customer contacts through internet marketing life insurance inquiries. A "fronter" may or may not need to be licensed depending on your state insurance law requirements.*

**Fronter:**
**Hi (Customer First Name). How are you today? Great to hear/Sorry to hear...**
**This is (Fronter's Name) from XYZ(Company Name) Final Expense Department.**

**I am fulfilling an inquiry regarding your request for more information on our current, state-approved benefits available in (Customer City) to pay your funeral and final expenses. To approve you for these low-cost life insurance plans, I am required by the state to pre-qualify you before you speak directly to a (Customer's State) Licensed Field Underwriter.**

**(Mr/Ms Customer Name), you gave us your Full Name as...Is this correct?**
**You gave us your correct address as....Is this correct? Super!**

**These permanent benefits are available to certain age groups. Were you born between (1938 and 2000)?** *[dates should reflect your carrier-specific age limits]* **Great! May I ask, what year were you born?..your D.O.B., please.**

**(Mr/Ms Customer Name), the plans we have today include No-Cost (FREE) Benefits. Your Licensed Field Underwriter can include them into your plan today. This will provide instant CASH Benefits to your loved ones at your passing. These are permanent CASH benefits, guaranteed to never decrease, and your rates will never go up, even if you live to be 100, or if your health changes. Your final expense protection is set for life after today.**

**Let's get a few preliminary questions out of the way before we speak directly to your Licensed Field Underwriter to know exactly what benefits you qualify for.**

**(Mr/Ms Customer Name), were you checking into benefits for yourself, or someone else?** *If "someone else" – STOP INTERVIEW – the buyer must be present.*

## ASK MEDICAL QUESTIONS:

*"Knock-Out" Questions are carrier-specific health questions that will disqualify a client for any coverage, if answered "Yes" to. Typical "Knock-Out" questions listed below are examples. Please, apply your own carrier-specific "Knock-Out" questions to this Lead Creation Script.*

> Have you ever been diagnosed with AIDS or HIV virus?
> Are you in a hospital or nursing home, or confined to a bed or wheelchair?
> Are you using oxygen equipment for respiratory assistance?
> Have you been diagnosed with Alzheimer's Disease or any dementia?
> Do you require professional assistance with Activities of Daily Living (ADL's): bathing, eating, or toileting? It is not very difficult to cover final expense health

**Thank you (Mr/Ms Customer Name) for your honesty. It does appear that you may qualify for state-approved CASH benefits.**

*> If customer does not qualify for a top plan due to poor health, simply transfer customer at this point to "Closing Agent" for Guarantee Issue product coverage.*

**You probably have some questions, so what we are going to do now is introduce you to the (Customer State) Licensed Field Underwriter on a secure line. He/She is a very nice person. They will answer all of your questions, serve your family for life, and show you just how inexpensive these plans are. By holding just a minute, I will make the connection for you.**

*Fronter puts customer on a brief hold, contacts Closing Agent.*

**Hi (Agent Name). I have (Mr/Ms Customer Name) on the line. He/She/They are interested in securing permanent, end-of-life protection for themselves at the lowest cost. Also, any Free Benefits that are available today would be helpful, ok?**

*Fronter adds customer to the call, and says goodbye to customer:*

**(Mr/Ms Customer Name), May I introduce you to (Agent Name)? He/She will be securing top benefits in your area for you and your family. It was nice speaking with you today. Thank you for allowing us to serve your family.**

*Fronter hangs up.*

*Customer call is transferred to "Closing Agent" [Five9 phone system is recommended]. Customer contact/health info, DOB, etc, should also be transferred now from "Fronter" to "Closing Agent."*

# LIVE Transfer Lead, "Closing Agent" Script

**Closing Agent: Final Expense Department, this is (<u>Agent First Name</u>). How may I help you?**

**Great, were you looking for information on the new life insurance plans available in (Customer's State) to pay your final expenses?**

**Ok, may I share with you who I am and exactly what I can do for you and your family?**

**I'm a Licensed Field Underwriter in (Customer's State). This means I'm not in a sales department. I'm a decision maker for people to qualify for our state regulated programs. The most important part of my job, while you have me on the phone today, is to make sure you understand exactly what your benefits are, how to apply for the benefits you qualify for, then to help you find the least expensive end-of-life plan to suit your needs. Is that what you were looking for? Great!**

**I'll need to ask some questions first. May I ask who I'm speaking with? Ok, and let's verify your address, city and state,.. your phone number,.. and date of birth.**

**(<u>Mr/Ms Customer Name</u>), these are new, low cost final expense plans that provide instant cash benefits to your loved ones as soon as you sign up. Unlike most plans, if you qualify, these are <u>PERMANENT</u> CASH benefits that will never decrease and your payments are guaranteed never to go up.**

**So, I must ask you a few more specific questions to see the exact level of benefits available to you.**

**Now, were you looking for benefits for yourself or someone else?**
*If "someone else" – STOP INTERVIEW – the buyer must be present.*

*The following 2 questions are to identify a real "Buyer" customer.*

1. **(Mr/Ms Customer Name), because these are specific plans for end of life benefits, do you currently have a permanent life insurance plan?**
   > *If 'Yes':* **Great! Most people do, I assume you are looking for some additional coverage due to the increase in funeral costs recently, or other reasons?**
   > *If 'No":* **Thank you for your honesty. Let's see what you qualify for. I promise to secure top benefits and make sure you and your family never have to worry about this again the rest of your life.**

   *A "No" answer here means to STOP the interview:*

2. **Because these are state regulated plans, you must have a real need in order to qualify. Do you feel that it's your responsibility to take care of your final expenses or your family's responsibility?**
   > *If My Responsibility:* **Perfect! We enjoy helping those who care about their family.**

**(<u>Customer</u> Name), one question. Without giving away any personal information, do you usually pay your bills by check, Visa/MasterCard, money order, or direct express?**
> *If Money Order – Stop Interview. No payments through mail.*
**(Mr/Ms Customer Name), anything but a money order will qualify you for a lower payment.** *Repeat previous question.*

**Ok, GREAT! It does appear initially that you may qualify for immediate cash benefits today. And, as you do qualify, many of these special plans start around a $1 a day. I just need to verify in a moment that this will fit into your budget.**

**Ok, now may I ask your height and weight, please?**
> *Access your carrier-specific Height-Weight Chart.*
> *If not within weight limits: Stop Interview, unless agent can offer a Guarantee Issue life insurance product.*

**EXAMPLES, Height-Weight Charts:** *Use your carrier-specific Height-Weight Chart here.*

### Final Expense Immediate Death Benefit

#### Maximum Weight Table (Unisex)

| Ht. | 4'11" | 5' | 5'1" | 5'2" | 5'3" | 5'4" | 5'5" | 5'6" | 5'7" |
|---|---|---|---|---|---|---|---|---|---|
| Wt. | 218 | 225 | 233 | 241 | 248 | 256 | 264 | 273 | 281 |

| Ht. | 5'8" | 5'9" | 5'10" | 5'11" | 6' | 6'1" | 6'2" | 6'3" | 6'4" |
|---|---|---|---|---|---|---|---|---|---|
| Wt. | 289 | 298 | 307 | 315 | 324 | 334 | 343 | 352 | 361 |

### Final Expense Graded Death Benefit For Applicable Plans
### Final Expense Return of Premium Benefit

#### Maximum Weight Table (Unisex)

| Ht. | 4'11" | 5' | 5'1" | 5'2" | 5'3" | 5'4" | 5'5" | 5'6" | 5'7" |
|---|---|---|---|---|---|---|---|---|---|
| Wt. | 238 | 246 | 254 | 262 | 271 | 280 | 288 | 297 | 306 |

| Ht. | 5'8" | 5'9" | 5'10" | 5'11" | 6' | 6'1" | 6'2" | 6'3" | 6'4" |
|---|---|---|---|---|---|---|---|---|---|
| Wt. | 316 | 325 | 335 | 344 | 354 | 364 | 374 | 384 | 394 |

### Final Expense ALL Plans

#### Minimum Weight Table (Unisex)

| Ht. | 4'11" | 5' | 5'1" | 5'2" | 5'3" | 5'4" | 5'5" | 5'6" | 5'7" |
|---|---|---|---|---|---|---|---|---|---|
| Wt. | 88 | 90 | 93 | 95 | 99 | 101 | 104 | 106 | 110 |

| Ht. | 5'8" | 5'9" | 5'10" | 5'11" | 6' | 6'1" | 6'2" | 6'3" | 6'4" |
|---|---|---|---|---|---|---|---|---|---|
| Wt. | 113 | 117 | 120 | 125 | 129 | 133 | 136 | 140 | 143 |

SAMPLE Height/Weight Chart:

| Height | Minimum Lbs | Maximum Lbs |
|---|---|---|
| 4' 11" | 86 | 227 |
| 5' 0" | 88 | 245 |
| 5' 1" | 90 | 256 |
| 5' 2" | 94 | 258 |
| 5' 3" | 98 | 269 |
| 5' 4" | 100 | 278 |
| 5' 5" | 102 | 290 |
| 5' 6" | 107 | 298 |
| 5' 7" | 109 | 302 |
| 5' 8" | 111 | 317 |
| 5' 9" | 115 | 330 |
| 5' 10" | 120 | 333 |
| 5' 11" | 129 | 344 |
| 6' 0" | 132 | 355 |
| 6' 1" | 134 | 362 |
| 6' 2" | 137 | 375 |
| 6' 3" | 142 | 388 |
| 6' 4" | 146 | 395 |

Go To **PreQualify Health** page of Dr. Clark's Sales Script MANUAL, follow succeeding script steps to..

# CLOSE THE SALE !!

# Predictive Lead, DIALER Script

*It is important to note while auto dialers [auto-dialer-voice-message] have been illegal on a federal level, some state-specific laws allow auto dialer usage. Please, contact FCC or your state Department of Insurance to gain clarification before lawfully utilizing an auto dialer in your state to generate leads. Predictive dialers [auto-dialer-no-voice-message] have been known to be legal on a federal level.*

*A sound dialer message should last no more than 25 seconds. You may adopt verbiage from the 3 options below to create your dialer message. Tailor your Predictive Lead Script to reflect your FE product age limits.*

3 Options:

## Option 1

This is an important announcement regarding your (Year, Ex: 2019) Federal Government death benefit of $255 to help with funeral and burial cost.

Decades ago, the Government's end-of-life death benefit of $255 may have been enough to cover basic funeral and burial expenses, but not now. Today, a typical funeral costs between $7,000 and $12,000. Cremation can go from $2,000 to $5,000. It falls upon a grieving family to pay for your uninsured funeral. Truth is, it is expensive to live. It is also expensive to die.

Now in your area, there is a state approved program in (Customer State) that can eliminate final expenses. It is a low cost state regulated whole life insurance plan that pays immediate cash for funeral and burial expenses even if you've been turned down for insurance in the past due to health problems. There's no physical exam, the rates will never go up, the benefits will never go down, and you'll never be cancelled regardless of age or health. You can be covered from day one!

Our programs start at under a dollar a day from one thousand to twenty five thousand dollars, so you only pay for the amount of coverage that you actually need. You can get more later, after you are qualified with a plan. If you would like more information, press the "1" key to hear what you may qualify for or you can press "9" to be removed from all future benefit updates. The information is free. Press the "1" key to see what you qualify for, that's the "1" key…press it now.

#1 Key Qualifier:
I'm sure by now; you may have questions. So if you are between the ages of 40 and 85 with an annual income between $10 and $40K you are almost pre-qualified for this low cost, state approved life insurance plan available in your area now. If you meet these requirements, congratulations and press "1" now to speak to a live field underwriter. Get all of your questions answered by our specialist. That's the "1" key, press it now.

## Option 2

Hi there. This is a very important message for people between the ages of 40 and 85.

Are you prepared for the final expense in your life? Most of us are not. It can leave a huge financial burden on our loved ones for funeral home and burial expenses.

What would you say if we could help qualify you for this rather inexpensive insurance for a very low cost regardless of your health? This is a limited time offer and is back by one of the largest final expense carriers.

To speak to a final expense representative, please Press "1" on your phone now. Or, press the "9" key to be taken off our list for future callings.

## Option 3

Hello. With the new stimulus package going into effect, state approved final benefits are approved in your area.

Are you between the ages of 40 and 85? You may be pre-approved for up to $50,000 in final expense life insurance. No medical exams are required to qualify and immediate coverage is available.

Press "1" to see what you qualify for. Press the "9" key to be removed from the list. Press the "1" key now.


*Upon pressing the #1 key, customer is immediate transferred LIVE to a licensed life insurance professional. See "Predictive Lead, Agent Script" on the next page..*

# Predictive Lead, AGENT Script

Final Expense Department, this is (Agent First Name). May I help you?

Were you looking for information on the new life insurance plan available in your state to pay final expenses?

Ok, may I share with you who I am and exactly what I can do for you and your family.

I'm a Licensed Field Underwriter in your state. That means that I'm the decision maker for people to qualify for these special state regulated plans. The most important part of my job, while you have me on the phone here today, is to make sure you understand exactly what your benefits are, how to apply for them if you indeed qualify and to help you find the least expensive benefit plan to suit your needs. Is this what you were looking for? Great!

I'll need to pre-qualify you first. May I ask who I'm speaking with? Ok, and let's verify your city and state. And your phone number.

Great, in order to qualify for these special plans, you must have been born between 1938 and 2000. So, what year were you born?..your D.O.B., please. Perfect!

(Mr/Ms Customer Name), these are the new, low cost final expense plans that provide instant cash benefits to your loved ones. Unlike most plans, if you qualify, these are PERMANENT benefits that will never decrease and your payments are guaranteed never to go up.

So, I do need to ask you a few preliminary questions to see if you meet the qualifications.

**Now, were you looking for benefits for yourself or someone else?**
*\* If "someone else" – STOP INTERVIEW – the buyer must be present.*

Ok, GREAT! And if you do qualify, many of these special plans start under $1 a day with additional FREE benefits as well. I just need to verify that this will fit into your budget. Now, let's cover some basic health questions to determine the levels of benefits you qualify for.

## Go To **PreQualify Health** page of Dr. Clark's Sales Script MANUAL, follow succeeding script steps to..

# CLOSE THE SALE !!

# Cold Call Lead

3 Options:

1. Hello, my name is (Agent Name). I am with a Final Expense Department in (Agent County). The reason for my call is we have recently completed a review of your community, and we have found that there are many families here that have considered a final expense policy but do not have enough information to make an informed decision. We have been providing final expense services to families in this community for the last __ years. We offer to review the specifics of our final expense plans to see if it would benefit you and your family the way it has benefited so many others in this area. One of our Licensed Field Underwriters is available to provide a no-cost review for you. Do have a few minutes?

* If lead is being generating to utilize later..
   - ✓ Secure contact info of customer.
   - ✓ Secure best time to contact customer.
   - ✓ Provide Confirmation # for "Consumer Safety Reasons". Put Confirmation # on agent lead.

---

Prior arrangement must be made with a funeral home:

2. Hi, my name is (Agent Name). I'm calling you on behalf of _____ Funeral Home. I have been helping families in your community since ____. We are conducting a Final Benefits Survey throughout (Customer City) to locate and identify families who were interested in pre-need funeral arrangements to relieve their loved ones of the emotional and financial burden that families will face at a time like this.
There are free benefits available in (Customer City) right now, for folks who respond and qualify for our Final Expense program. At my Final Expense Department, we thrive on giving our clients the personal service they deserve. Our Licensed Field Underwriter is available. Do you have a few minutes?

   - ✓ Collect same customer information as the previous lead script.

---

3. Hi, (Customer Name). This is (Agent Name) at a Final Expense Department. The reason for my call - we are providing a FREE review with one of our Licensed Field Underwriters, as a service to your community to be able to access our Final Benefits here. We are trying to "get the word out" about FREE benefits available in (Customer City) right now, for those who respond and qualify for one of our Final Benefit Plans that cover your funeral and burial expenses for life. Our state-Licensed Field Underwriter is available (today/this week). Do you have a few minutes?

   - ✓ Collect same customer information as the previous lead script.

# Appointment Setting Lead

Hi, (<u>Customer First Name</u>)!

This is (<u>Agent Name</u>)'s office with (<u>Company Name</u>). The reason for my call is, you recently sent a card back / made an inquiry, requesting more information about our final benefit plans. The card/advertisement briefly mentioned about plans you might qualify for. So, I just wanted to call and verify the information here you have given us. Our records indicate that you have not received the free information.

Your full name is _____. You spell it -------. Is this correct?
You gave us your date of birth as being_____. Is that correct?
Your correct mailing address is _____. Is that you?
Great.

(<u>Customer Name</u>), when the card/inquiry was sent back, it was filled out for (you / both of you). Were you primarily concerned with benefits on yourself, or did you have others in mind? OK, great.

(<u>Customer Name</u>), we do have that information available for you this week. This is a state regulated program in the state of (<u>Customer State</u>) with immediate benefits. Since there is no physical exam, the guidelines here ask that we see you in person to cover a few basic health questions to see what you qualify for. We have a nice representative in your area in (<u>Customer City</u>) all day on (<u>Day of week</u>) this week.
What would be better for you, mornings or afternoons? Is (time) o'clock ok? Great.

The rep. who will be visiting with you, his/her name is (<u>Agent Name</u>). If you have a little piece of paper, could you jot down the name, so you won't forget about him? His name is (<u>Agent Name</u>). You spell it ------. He's a super nice fella', and we are looking at (time o'clock) on (<u>Day of week</u>) to deliver the free quote information for you. He'll show you exactly the approved benefits you may qualify for. (<u>Agent Name</u>) will be glad to help you every way that he can. OK?

We'll see you then at (time o'clock) on (<u>Day of week</u>).

Thank you (<u>Customer Name</u>). Have a blessed day. Bye.

*Optional* : (<u>Agent Name</u>) will have your card with him that you mailed in, so you can see it.

# Voicemail Lead

*A lead is generated when any caller to your company responds on your voicemail. A strategic outgoing voicemail message captures a lead when an interested customer leaves a message.*

*Keep the confirmation number short, Ex: 3321.*

*When returning a call, be sure to ask for customer's "confirmation number" to make your follow up call officially verified. When returning a call, have your Appointment Setting Script ready to create a field agent lead, or your Sales Script MANUAL ready for an immediate phone sale.*

Your Outgoing Voicemail Message:

WELCOME TO THE <u>FINAL EXPENSE DEPARTMENT</u>.
(or <u>Senior Benefits Dept</u>, or <u>American Benefits Dept</u>, or <u>Final Benefits Dept</u>, etc..)

UNFORTUNATELY,
ALL OF OUR LICENSED REPRESENTATIVES
ARE CURRENTLY BUSY ASSISTING OTHERS.

YOUR CALL IS VERY IMPORTANT.
WE RETURN ALL CALLS AS SOON AS POSSIBLE.

PLEASE WRITE DOWN YOUR CONFIRMATION NUMBER.

TO SECURE AVAILABLE BENEFITS, YOUR
CONFIRMATION NUMBER IS: -----.

PLEASE HAVE YOUR CONFIRMATION NUMBER -----,
WHEN WE CALL TO CONFIRM AVAILABLE BENEFITS.

AT THE TONE, PLEASE STATE YOUR NAME CLEARLY,
& PHONE NUMBER WITH AREA CODE SLOWLY.

A LICENSED REPRESENTATIVE WILL CONTACT YOU SOON
IN THE ORDER YOUR CALL WAS RECEIVED.

AGAIN, YOUR CONFIRMATION NUMBER IS -----.

# Answering Machine Agent Phone Message

*If your prospect customer is not home. Leave a message that prompts a return phone call. When leaving a message, pronounce your **name/phone number** s-l-o-w-l-y and clearly!*
*YYYY = incorrect year of birth (this is the 'hook' that generates a return phone call!)*

------------------
**1st Answering Machine Phone Message:**

Hi, this is (<u>Agent Name</u>) at "<u>your company name, final benefits department</u>" leaving a message for Mr.,Ms. (<u>Customer Name</u>). Mr.,Ms. (<u>Customer Name</u>), you requested our (current year, Ex: 2019) Senior Benefit Update that we are trying to get out to you. You gave us your Date of Birth as, M/D/YR,..or YYYY, I'm not sure which it is, but this does affect the level of benefits you may qualify for there in (<u>Customer City</u>). Please, contact us as soon as you can, so we can get the correct information out to you today.

The direct line to my desk is ---.---.----.  Again, this is (<u>Agent Name</u>). Have a good day.

*\*Note: Mention both a correct **and** incorrect year of the customer's birth in your message.*

---------------
**2nd Answering Machine Phone Message**: *\*Approx. 2-5 business days between leaving phone messages.*

Hi, this message is for (<u>Customer Name</u>). I am (<u>Agent Name</u>) with benefits information you requested here at my department available right now in (<u>Customer City</u>). The Date of Birth you gave us is either M/D/YR,..or YYYY. Please, let my secretary know which one is correct, so that we can get the correct information out to you as soon as possible.

Our direct Toll Free number is ---.---.----.  Have a blessed day!

---------------
**3rd Answering Machine Phone Message:** *\*This message should only be utilized as a very last resort.*

Hi, this is (<u>Agent Name</u>) at a "final benefits department" with a final message. I have left several phone messages for (<u>Customer Name</u>). Our records indicate he/she has not responded to the No-cost information requested here at my department. There are state-regulated cash benefits available for folks who respond and qualify. This is my final offer, if I do not hear back immediately from (<u>Customer Name</u>).
---.---.---- is the number to my desk.  Thank you.  Again, this is my final offer.

# Publications by Dr. Troy Clark

*amazon.com/author/troyclark*

Dr. Troy Clark is America's original final expense insurance author, "**How YOU Can Master Final Expense**" (2010).

Troy's blockbuster book has energized multitudes of business professionals, providing hope and practical know-how to succeed. His field-tested methods released salespersons who were living on food stamps to earning weekly 4 figure paychecks within 10 weeks. Troy averaged 14 sales per week acquiring 669 clients in his first year (48 weeks) to launch an exceptional life insurance career in 2003. He is one of the select few awarded National Top Producers for both field sales and phone sales in final expense life insurance.

Those who hear him speak say that Troy is a motivator who will pick you up and take you farther than you ever dreamed. He's a balanced man of faith, vision, and patriotism, with a passion to see others succeed. Troy possess a rare talent, while building his own career, he builds "successful people", who become winners in life themselves. A commoner among insurance professionals, Troy is personable and accessible to speak for small or large adult groups/events.

Proceeds from Troy's publications provide financial assistance to homeless shelters, crisis pregnancy centers, and treatment centers for victims of abuse, as well as faith-based organizations and charities.

Utilized in Fortune 500 corporations, college level curriculum, newspaper and magazine articles, start-up businesses, TV and Radio program content, consumed by sales professionals, as well as circulated among military officers and troops overseas, Dr. Troy Clark's success life-principles are woven into the fabric of US and international society.

# NOTES

## NOTES

# NOTES

# **NOTES**

# **NOTES**

www.ingramcontent.com/pod-product-compliance
Lightning Source LLC
Chambersburg PA
CBHW081653220526
45468CB00009B/2633